1000

STICKERS FOR GIRLS

Pull out the sticker sheets and have them with you when you complete each page. There are also lots of extra stickers to use in this book or anywhere you like!

Designed by Katie Cox

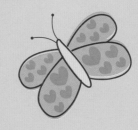

make
believe
ideas

Fairy dress designer!

Complete the design then add patterns and stickers to create your very own fairy dress!

Add WINGS to things!

Add wings to these pictures!

WOW! A flying bunny!

Create a flying fairy cupcake!

Can I have fairy wings please!

Look at my beautiful wings!

4

Look on the sticker page for cakes and treats!

Fun fairy cupcakes

Draw a big cupcake here and add stickers to make it look totally tasty!

FLOUR

Whose fairy footprints are in the flour?

Top this cupcake with tempting treats.

Find stickers of more yummy cupcakes.

Fairy shopping list

If you were a fairy, what would you buy? Write or draw your favorite things.

Finish the fairy shopping list!

Find stickers to fit these shapes.

I need an ...

pple

and some ...

ing

and a ...

and

and some ...

eg s

6

What's in the bag?

Find and place stickers for the fairy's shopping bag.

Fairy numbers

Design your own fairy numbers!

0 1 2 3 4 5

This one has wings!

Practice drawing
fairies here!

Color trails

Find the stickers, then follow the trails to discover which garden friend has been nibbling the flowers!

summertime garden

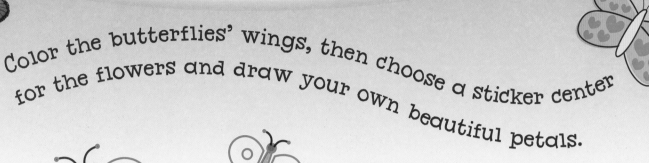

Color the butterflies' wings, then choose a sticker center for the flowers and draw your own beautiful petals.

Who is in the nest?

You'll find them on the sticker page.

Find **3** eggs to go in here.

Find **2** birds to sit in the nest!

Draw a big bird in this nest.

12

summertime tree

Turn winter into summer by adding sticker leaves, apples, birds, butterflies, and your own patterns to this tree.

13

BUZZY BEE's flower fun

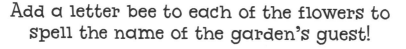

Add a letter bee to each of the flowers to
spell the name of the garden's guest!

The bees are playing in the sunflowers. Circle the one that doesn't match!

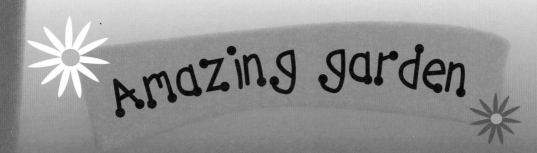

Amazing garden

Look through the window. What do you see?
Draw your own amazing garden here.

Beautiful bouquet

Decorate the vase then fill it with beautiful flowers!

Princess castle

Complete the princess castle, then fill the garden with beautiful stickers.

Draw a flag here!

Find a princess to go here!

Find a big window to stick here.

Draw a big door and add some stickers!

Princess Wardrobe

Help Princess Penny organize her wardrobe! ⭐ ⭐

Find 2 tops to stick here.

Find some striped gloves to go here.

Draw a new dress here.

Find 2 bags and 1 hat to go here.

Add some fluffy shoes.

Picnic with a Princess!

Find the colored bubbles to match
Princess Polly's favorite drinks!

Orange juice

Apple juice

Grape juice

Princess Penny dropped her basket and has broken all the cookies in two!
Find the matching pieces and line them up.

Invitation to a Grand Ball

Little Princess Polly has been invited to a ball. Join the dots to complete her dress and then decorate it with stickers and your own designs.

Colorful crowns to decorate!

Decorate these beautiful crowns using different shapes.

sleeping princess

Color a beautiful quilt for the little princess and add stickers!

Use stickers to place some toys under her bed!

Princess Poppy's birthday party!

There is lots to do for Poppy's party. Can you help her?

Draw a special princess hat!

Decorate the gift!

Find some perfect princess slippers.

Sticker some candles on the cupcake. How old is she?

Practice drawing princesses here!

PuPPy Play!

Find stickers for each pet then, guess which puppy has found the ball.

How many puppies are there on this page?

Pet Pals

Design and decorate beautiful baskets for these pet pals.

toy tangle

10 toy mice are tangled up in the wool. Find stickers for the kittens, then find the mice.

Birthday surprise!

Find stickers for the gifts, then draw a ribbon to match the pets to their perfect present.

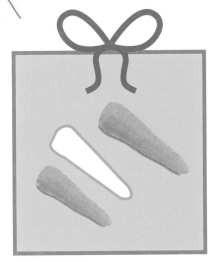

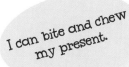

I can bite and chew my present.

I can play with my present!

I got just what I needed!

29

where are our babies?

Fill in this section!

Sticker my baby here!

I am a

uppy

Sticker 2 of my babies here!

We are

i lets

Sticker my 4 babies here!

We are

d klings

Sticker my baby here!

I am a

alf

Sticker a group of my babies here!

We are

itten

Animal patterns

Decorate these animals with crazy patterns and stickers.

Odd one out

The farmyard friends are on their way to the pond.
Find stickers for the missing cuties
and circle the one that doesn't match!

Practice drawing
cute animals
and pets here!

Mermaid necklaces

Find stickers for the missing shapes to complete the pattern.

The mermaids have broken their necklaces! Help fix them by adding the missing parts.

34

Be a mermaid

Draw yourself as a beautiful mermaid.

Decorate the frame with stickers!

Mermaid sleepover

Mermaid Miriam is going to a sleepover. What is she taking with her?

Try to complete the names of these objects.

I am taking my... and

oothbrush   to th aste

What did Miriam forget? Find the sticker!

I need my...

hairb ush

I forgot my...

eddy b ar

Fishy fun!

Fill this scene with beautiful fish and your own drawings, then find the 9 sea shells!

38

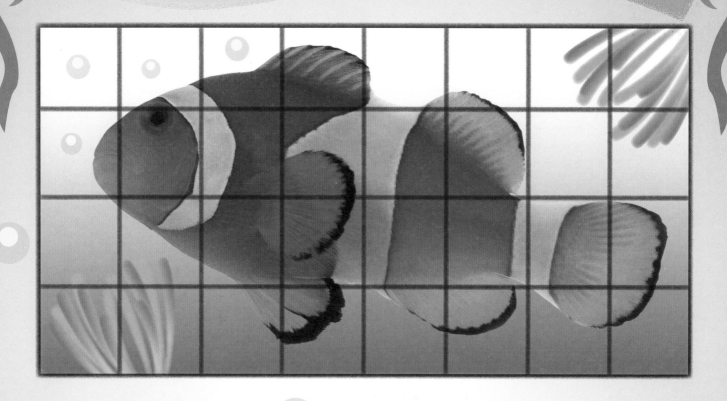

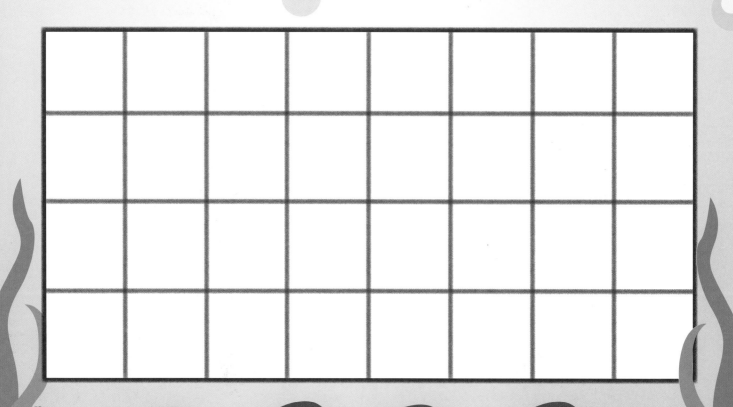

Stickers for pages 2 & 3

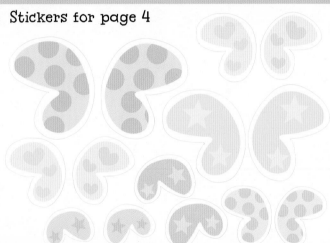

Stickers for page 4

Stickers for page 5

Stickers for page 6

Stickers for page 7

Stickers for pages 9, 10 & 11

Stickers for page 12

Stickers for page 13

Stickers for page 14

Stickers for page 16

Stickers for page 17

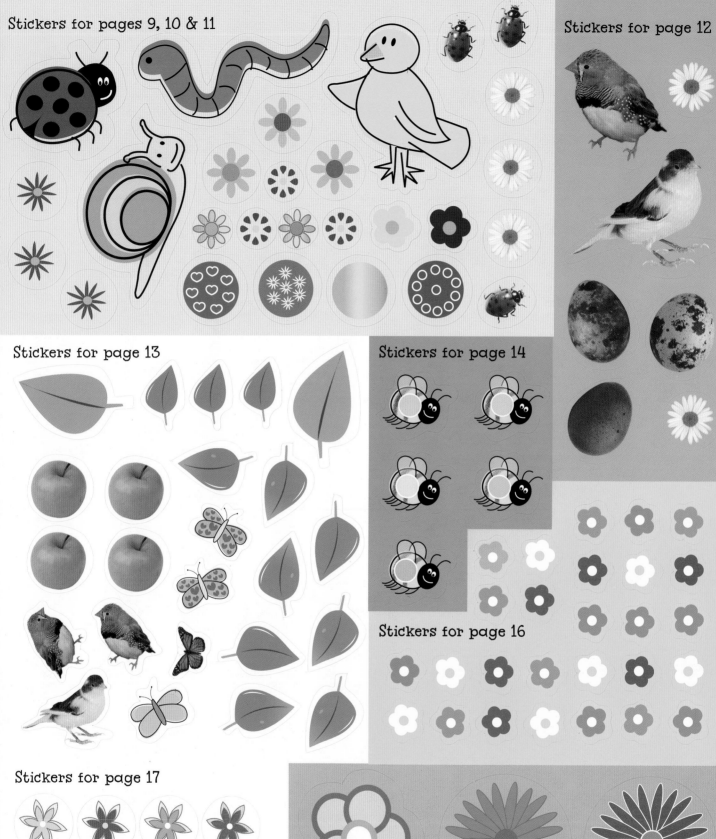

Stickers for page 18

Stickers for page 19

Stickers for page 20

Stickers for pages 21 & 22

Stickers for page 23

Stickers for page 24

Stickers for page 25

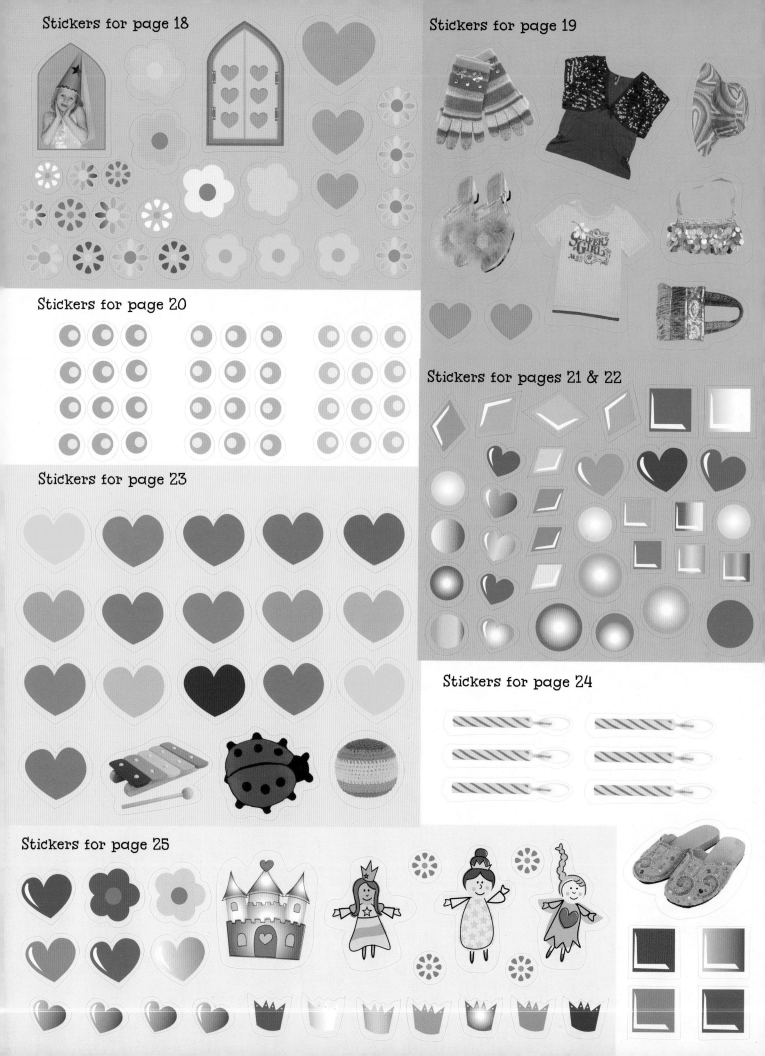

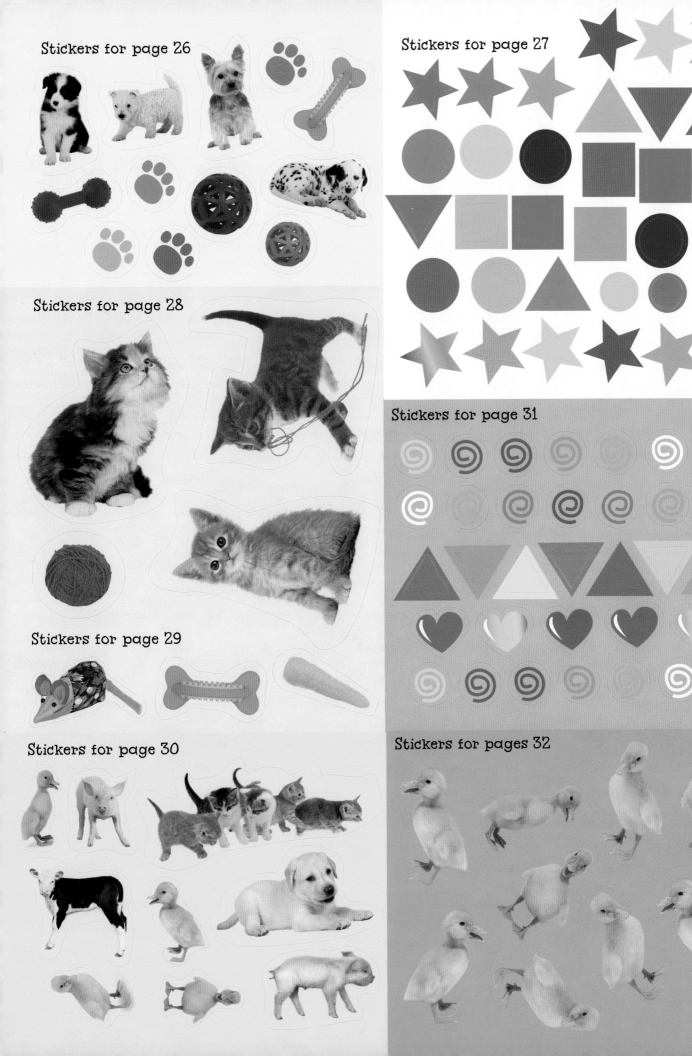

Stickers for page 26

Stickers for page 27

Stickers for page 28

Stickers for page 29

Stickers for page 30

Stickers for page 31

Stickers for pages 32

Stickers for page 34

Stickers for page 35

Stickers for page 36

Stickers for page 37

Stickers for pages 38 & 39